SANJEEV KAPOOR

Simple Home Baking

In association with Alyona Kapoor

Popular Prakashan
www.popularprakashan.com

Published by
POPULAR PRAKASHAN PVT. LTD.
301, Mahalaxmi Chambers
22, Bhulabhai Desai Road
Mumbai - 400 026
for KHANA KHAZANA PUBLICATIONS PVT. LTD.

First Published 2009
Fourth Reprint August 2014

(4323)
ISBN: 978-81-7991-575-2

Design: Anjali Sawant

PRINTED IN INDIA
by Saurabh Printers Pvt. Ltd.
A-16, Sector 4, Noida

AUTHOR'S NOTE

This collection of simple baking recipes is in response to a request from many of my readers who look at baking as a complicated process, which is inevitably doomed to failure, unless one is armed with the most sophisticated equipment and years of experience.

Let me assure you that while baking, unlike cooking, does demand precision in weights and measures, and the following of steps in a prescribed process, the end result is satisfaction guaranteed. I have written the recipes in a simple easy-to-follow manner so that a novice will achieve the same result as a professional chef. All you need is your enthusiasm, an oven and this book close at hand, and you will be able to whip up culinary masterpieces in your own kitchen, which will soon be perfumed with the heavenly aroma of freshly baked cakes, cookies and pies.

Here are a few tips that will ensure you achieve baking perfection:

1. To grease baking tins, rub the base and sides with a piece of paper towel or napkin smeared with a small quantity of fat. Use the baking tin size specified in the recipe.

2. Fill cake tins no more than half full to allow for rising during baking.
3. Use standard measuring spoons and measuring cups. Do not use regular spoons and tea or coffee cups or mugs to measure ingredients for baking recipes as it is important to be exact.
4. Always stir flour to "loosen" before measuring.
5. To measure dry ingredients including flours, corn flour, cocoa, granulated and powdered sugars, spoon dry ingredients into the correct-size cups until they are overflowing.
6. Level the surface with the straight edge of a spatula or knife.
7. Use a glass or plastic transparent measuring jug with a spout to measure all liquid amounts greater than 1 cup.
8. Make sure all ingredients are at room temperature (unless otherwise specified) for best results.
9. Always sift flour, soda bicarbonate, baking powder, salt and spices to avoid lumps.
10. Do not over beat the ingredients. Scrape the sides and bottom of bowl frequently with a rubber spatula during mixing.
11. Make sure the oven preheats for at least 20 minutes before using.
12. Avoid opening the oven door during baking.

13. When a cake is done, it will give out a strong buttery aroma, It should be golden brown in colour and will shrink slightly from the sides of the tin. The top of the cake will spring back when pressed lightly.
14. To test for doneness, insert a long thin skewer into the centre of the cake - if it comes out clean, without any batter clinging to it, it is done.
15. Biscuits and cookies should be pale gold on top and golden brown on the bottom.
16. Ice cakes or biscuits when they are completely cooled, or the icing will melt or slide off the cake.

Some Baking Terms

Bake blind: To bake an unfilled pastry case. Prick the pastry case with a fork to prevent puffing. Cover with aluminum foil or greaseproof paper and fill with rice or beans. Bake for about 10 to 15 minutes.

Double-boiler: The ingredients are put into a pan or a heatproof bowl placed over a pan of gently simmering water and cooked, stirring continuously, till the desired consistency is reached.

Happy Baking!

CONTENTS

CAKES

COOKIES

CHOCOLATE BROWNIES

Ingredients

100 grams dark cooking chocolate

1 cup refined flour

1 teaspoon baking powder

90 grams butter

¾ cup caster sugar

2 eggs

1 teaspoon vanilla essence

½ cup walnut halves, chopped

Method

1. Preheat an oven to 180°C/350°F/ Gas Mark 4.
2. Grease an eight-inch square baking tin. Sift together the flour and baking powder.
3. Melt the chocolate and butter in a double-boiler, or in a large microwave-safe bowl, uncovered, in the microwave oven on HIGH (100%) for one minute.

4. Beat in the sugar, eggs and vanilla essence and blend well.

5. Add the sifted flour and walnuts and mix well.

6. Pour the mixture into the tin and bake for forty-five minutes.

4. Place on a wire rack to cool. Cut into squares and serve.

Makes 16 brownies

DATE AND WALNUT CAKE

Ingredients

1½ cups (200 grams) seedless dates, finely chopped

¾ cup walnut kernels, finely chopped

1 cup refined flour

½ cup sugar

¾ cup butter

3 eggs, lightly beaten

¾ teaspoon soda bicarbonate

Icing sugar for decoration

Method

1. Preheat oven to 110°C/225°F/ Gas Mark ¼. Grease a cake tin. Mix the sugar, butter and chopped dates with half a cup of lukewarm water.
2. Sift the flour and soda bicarbonate together and stir in the chopped walnuts. Mix the flour and date mixture together well. Add the beaten eggs and mix thoroughly.
3. Pour the mixture into the greased cake tin and bake for thirty to forty minutes. Remove and sprinkle with icing sugar. Slice and serve warm.

PINEAPPLE GÂTEAU

Ingredients

1 eight-inch round Sponge Cake (page 88, 89 or 90)

6 tinned pineapple slices

½ cup pineapple syrup

1½ cups thick cream, whipped

Method

1. Reserve one slice of pineapple for decoration and chop the rest.
2. Halve the sponge cake horizontally. Place the halves on a flat surface with the cut surface facing upward.
3. Sprinkle a little pineapple syrup from the tin over each half.
4. Place the chopped pineapple in a bowl; add a little whipped cream and mix well.
5. Spread the mixture on one half of the cake. Cover with the second half.

6. Place the cake on a plate. Spread the remaining whipped cream smoothly over the top and the sides with a palette knife dipped in hot water.

7. Cut the reserved pineapple slice in cubes and use to decorate the gâteau. Chill in a refrigerator till ready to serve.

Makes one 8-inch gâteau

Note: Use the syrup that comes with the pineapple slices in the can.

BLACK FOREST GÂTEAU

Ingredients

½ cup refined flour

2 tablespoons cocoa powder

3 eggs

6 tablespoons sugar

1 teaspoon baking powder

¼ cup milk

½ cup tinned cherries

1 cup whipping cream

Chocolate curls

Method

1. Preheat an oven to 180°C/350°F/ Gas Mark 4. Line the base and grease a deep eight-inch round cake tin.

2. Beat together the eggs and sugar for eight to ten minutes, or until thick and pale. Sift the flour and cocoa over the egg mixture and fold in gently, adding the milk as you mix.

3. Transfer the batter to the cake tin. Bake for thirty minutes, or until springy to the touch. Remove from the oven and

leave the cake in the tin for five minutes to cool slightly. Turn out onto a wire rack, peel off the paper base and leave to cool.

4. Cut the cake in half horizontally and sprinkle each half with cherry syrup from the tinned cherries. Whip the cream until stiff. Place the bottom half of cake on a serving plate and spread half the whipped cream over it. Cover with the top half of the cake. Use the remaining cream to cover the top and sides.

5. Decorate the gâteau with chocolate curls and cherries and chill in the refrigerator.

Makes one 8-inch gâteau

BANANA LOAF CAKE
(Banana Bread)

Ingredients

2 cups mashed overripe bananas

2 cups refined flour

1 teaspoon soda bicarbonate

¼ teaspoon salt

100 grams butter

¾ cup demerara sugar

2 eggs, beaten

Method

1. Preheat an oven to 180°C/350°F/ Gas Mark 4. Lightly grease a nine-inch by five-inch loaf tin.
2. Sift the flour, soda bicarbonate and salt together. Cream the butter and demerara sugar together in a bowl.
3. In a separate bowl, mix the eggs and mashed bananas until well blended.

4. Combine the flour, creamed mixture and the egg and banana mixture together gently.
5. Pour the batter into the loaf tin and bake for fifty to sixty minutes, or until a toothpick inserted into the centre of the loaf comes out clean.
6. Remove from the oven and leave to cool in the tin for ten minutes; turn out onto a wire rack to cool. Slice and serve.

Makes one 9-inch by 5-inch loaf

ORANGE MARMALADE CAKE

Ingredients

½ cup orange marmalade

2 teaspoons grated orange rind

¼ cup orange juice

2½ cups refined flour

2½ teaspoons baking powder

150 grams butter

¾ cup sugar

3 eggs, separated

⅓ cup tutti-frutti

½ cup milk

Orange Icing

60 grams butter

2 teaspoons grated orange rind

½ cup powdered sugar, sifted

1 tablespoon orange juice

Method

1. Preheat the oven to 150°C/300°F/Gas Mark 2. Grease and line an eight-inch square cake tin. Sift the flour and baking powder together.

2. Cream the butter, orange rind, sugar and egg yolks in a small bowl with an electric mixer on medium speed, or with a whisk until light and fluffy.

3. Stir in the marmalade and tutti-frutti. Fold in the sifted flour alternately with the milk and orange juice. Beat the egg whites until they form firm peaks and fold gently into the cake mixture.

4. Pour the batter into the prepared tin and bake in the preheated oven for thirty-five minutes.

5. Remove from the oven and transfer to a wire rack to cool.

6. To make the orange icing, cream the butter and orange rind in a bowl.

7. Gradually beat in the sifted powdered sugar and orange juice. Spread the cooled cake with the icing. Cut into slices and serve.

Makes one (750 grams) 8-inch square cake

CHOCOLATE ÉCLAIRS

Ingredients

Pastry

¾ cup refined flour

A pinch of salt

75 grams chilled butter, diced

3 eggs, beaten

Filling

1 cup whipping cream

Chocolate icing

50 grams dark chocolate

25 grams unsalted butter

Method

1. Preheat an oven to 200°C/400°F/Gas Mark 6. Sift the flour with salt.

2. Place the butter and one cup of water in a pan and stir over low heat until the butter melts. Add the flour all at once and stir over medium heat until the mixture forms a ball and leaves the sides of the pan. Place the mixture in a bowl and cool slightly. Beat in the eggs, one at a time, until the dough is smooth and shiny. Spoon the

mixture into a piping bag with a wide nozzle. Fold down the top of the bag to squeeze the dough to the bottom.

3. Line two flat baking trays with greaseproof paper. Squeeze the mixture into medium-sized sausage shapes well apart onto the baking tray, as the éclairs will double in size in the oven. Bake for about thirty minutes. Remove from the oven when the éclairs are puffed and golden brown and feel hard when tapped. Immediately take each éclair off the baking sheet (they will be very hot, so wear oven gloves) and, with the point of a knife, gently slit the top to let out the steam and to prevent the éclairs from becoming soggy. Transfer to a wire rack to cool and dry out.

4. For the filling, whip the cream in a small bowl until it is just thick enough to hold its shape. Place it in the refrigerator while you make the chocolate icing. For the icing, melt the chocolate in a double-boiler, or in a microwave-safe bowl in the microwave oven on HIGH (100%) for one minute.

5. Stir in the butter till well mixed. Fill the inside of each éclair with

whipped cream using a piping bag with a small nozzle. Dip the top of each éclair into the sauce. Leave the éclairs on the wire rack until the icing has set.

6. In the unlikely event that you are not going to eat them straight away, you can put them in the refrigerator for a few hours!

Makes 14 éclairs

TEATIME CARDAMOM CAKE

Ingredients

1 cup refined flour

½ teaspoon baking powder

1 teaspoon green cardamom powder

3 eggs

½ cup caster sugar

1 teaspoon vanilla essence

½ cup butter + for greasing

2 tablespoons milk

Method

1. Sieve the flour, baking powder and green cardamom powder into a bowl.

2. Grease a cake tin and set aside.

3. Break the eggs into another bowl. Add the sugar and beat till sugar mixes properly. Add the vanilla essence and mix.

4. Add the flour mixture to the egg mixture and mix well.

5. Heat a pressure cooker and place a base in it.
6. Melt half a cup of butter in a microwave oven (or directly on gas). Add to the batter and mix. And the milk and mix.
7. Pour the batter into the greased cake tin and place it in the pressure cooker.
8. Remove the gasket and cover the cooker. Cook for thirty to thirty five minutes without the weight.
9. When done remove from the cooker and cool.
10. Slice and serve.

SWISS ROLL

Ingredients

¾ cup refined flour

½ teaspoon baking powder

4 eggs, separated

¾ cup powdered sugar, sifted

1 teaspoon vanilla essence

¼ teaspoon salt

5 tablespoons mixed fruit jam

2 teaspoons caster sugar, for dusting

Method

1. Preheat an oven to 190°C/375°F/Gas Mark 5. Line a fifteen-inch by ten-inch baking tray with greased thick unglazed brown paper.

2. Sift the flour together with the baking powder. Beat the egg yolks until light; continue beating the mixture, adding the sugar gradually, till creamy. Stir in the vanilla essence.

3. Gently and gradually fold the flour into the egg mixture. Beat the batter until smooth. Whip the egg whites with salt until stiff, but not dry. Fold the egg whites lightly into the cake batter.

4. Spread the batter in the prepared tray and bake for about twelve minutes. While still hot, turn the cake out onto a sheet of greaseproof paper, sprinkled with icing sugar.

5. Trim the hard edges. Spread the cake with jam and carefully roll it up. Wrap the roll in the butter paper. Cut into slices and serve.

Makes one 400 grams Swiss Roll

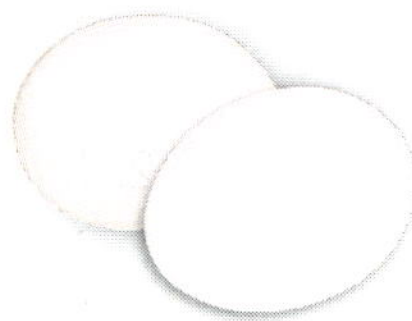

PINEAPPLE UPSIDE-DOWN CAKE

Ingredients

Topping

8 tinned pineapple slices, drained

50 grams butter, softened

1 cup demerara sugar

Cake

1 cup refined flour

1 teaspoon baking powder

3 eggs, separated

100 grams butter, softened

1 teaspoon vanilla essence

1 cup powdered sugar, sifted

½ cup milk

Method

1. Preheat an oven to 190°C/375°F/ Gas Mark 5. Grease and line a nine-inch round cake tin.
2. Mix the butter and demerara sugar and spread it in at the bottom of the cake tin. Arrange

a layer of pineapple slices over the butter-sugar mixture.

3. For the cake batter, sift together the flour and baking powder. Beat the egg yolks in a small bowl; mix in the butter and vanilla essence.

4. Whisk the egg whites until stiff but not dry. Fold in the sifted sugar one tablespoonful at a time. Fold the egg yolk mixture into the egg whites; fold in the sifted flour, one-fourth cupful at a time.

5. Pour the batter over the pineapple slices in the tin and bake for about half an hour. Allow to cool a little before removing from the tin. Turn the cake upside down onto a serving dish with the glazed pineapple slices on top.

Makes one 9-inch cake

CARROT CAKE

Ingredients

3-4 medium carrots, grated

3 tablespoons oil + for greasing

1 medium apple

1/3 cup orange juice

1 egg

2 tablespoon sugar

1½ cups refined flour

½ teaspoon baking powder

½ teaspoon soda bicarbonate

1 teaspoon cinnamon powder

Method

1. Preheat an oven to 180°C/350°F/ Gas Mark 4. Grease an eight-inch round cake tin with oil.
2. Grate the apple into a bowl; add the carrots and orange juice and mix.
3. Break the egg into the bowl and mix well. Stir in the sugar.
4. Sieve together the flour, baking powder, soda bicarbonate and cinnamon powder into the bowl and mix gently. Add oil and mix.

5. Pour the batter into the greased tin and bake in the preheated oven for approximately thirty minutes.

6. Turn out the cake onto a wire rack to cool.

7. Cut into slices and serve.

Makes one (1 kg) 8-inch cake

FRUIT CAKE

Ingredients

1½ cups refined flour

1½ teaspoons baking powder

¼ teaspoon salt

1 teaspoon cinnamon powder

120 grams butter

2 ⅔ tablespoon sugar

1 teaspoon orange zest

¼ cup orange juice

½ cup raisins (kishmish)

½ cup currants

50 grams glazed cherries, chopped

1 tablespoon orange marmalade

2 eggs, whisked

Method

1. Preheat the oven to 170°C/325°F/Gas Mark 3. Grease an eight-inch round cake tin.
2. Sift together the flour, baking powder, salt and cinnamon powder into a large bowl. Place

the butter, sugar, orange zest, orange juice and two-third cup of water into a pan. Cook over low heat until the mixture is smooth.

3. Stir in the raisins and currants and continue to simmer for another five minutes.

4. Cool. Pour the butter mixture into the sifted flour and mix well.

5. Mix in the glazed cherries, orange marmalade and eggs.

6. Pour the batter into the greased tin and bake for one-and-a-half hours till a toothpick inserted into the centre comes out clean. Cool the cake in the tin.

Makes one 8-inch cake

MAWA CUPCAKES

Ingredients

1½ cups refined flour

1½ tablespoons mawa, crumbled

150 grams butter, softened

¾ cup powdered sugar

5 tablespoons milk powder

2 tablespoons cornflour

1 teaspoon baking powder

1 teaspoon soda bicarbonate

¼ teaspoon green cardamom powder

¼ cup buttermilk

2 tablespoons milk

Method

1. Preheat an oven to 180°C/350°F/ Gas Mark 4. Grease twelve moulds or paper cups.

2. Cream the butter and powdered sugar in a bowl with a wooden spoon till light and fluffy. Sift the milk powder into the bowl and

continue to mix. Add the mawa and mix again. Sift the flour, cornflour, baking powder, soda bicarbonate and cardamom powder together into the bowl and mix. Add the buttermilk to adjust the consistency. If the batter is still too thick add a little milk and mix.

3. Pour the batter into the greased moulds or paper cups. Tap the moulds lightly to level the batter. Bake for thirty minutes. Remove from the oven and place on a wire rack to cool before unmoulding.
4. Serve warm or cold.

Makes 12 cupcakes

CHOCOLATE CUPCAKES

Ingredients

1¾ cups refined flour

60 grams dark cooking chocolate, chopped

100 grams butter

1½ cups powdered sugar, sifted

4 eggs, separated

3 teaspoons baking powder

¼ teaspoon salt

½ cup milk

2 teaspoons vanilla essence

Icing sugar for dusting

Method

1. Preheat an oven to 180°C/350°F/ Gas Mark 4. Grease 16 moulds or paper cups.

2. Melt the chocolate in a double-boiler and stir in five tablespoons of boiling water. Cool slightly.

3. Beat the butter until soft and gradually add the sugar. Beat until very light and creamy. Beat in one egg yolk at a time. Add the melted chocolate and mix well.

4. Sift the flour with the baking powder and salt. Mix together the milk and vanilla essence.

5. Add the flour mixture and milk alternately to the creamed mixture in three parts, beating well after each addition.

6. Whip the egg whites till stiff but not dry; fold lightly into the cake batter.

7. Pour the batter into the moulds or paper cups till two-third full and bake in the preheated oven for thirty minutes.

8. Cool on a wire rack before turning out of the moulds.

9. Sprinkle with icing sugar and serve.

Makes 16 cupcakes

ZESTY LEMON CAKE

Ingredients

Grated rind of 1 lemon

3 tablespoons lemon juice

1¾ cups refined flour

1 teaspoon soda bicarbonate

2 teaspoons baking powder

100 grams butter + for greasing

½ cup powdered sugar

1¼ cups yogurt

Topping

3 tablespoons lemon juice

3 tablespoons sugar

Method

1. Sift together the flour, soda bicarbonate and baking powder into a bowl. In a separate bowl, cream together the butter and powdered sugar.

2. Add the yogurt, lemon rind and lemon juice and mix well. Add

the flour, a little at a time, and fold into the batter.

3. Heat a pressure cooker with some water and place a perforated plate in it.
4. Grease an eight-inch cake tin lightly with butter and pour the cake batter into the tin.
5. Place the tin on the base in the pressure cooker. Remove the gasket and cover the cooker with the lid without the weight.
6. Cook for thirty to thirty-five minutes. Remove when done.
7. For the topping, place the sugar and three tablespoons of water into a pan and heat till the sugar dissolves.
8. Stir in the lemon juice. Pour the syrup over the hot cake. Cool the cake in the tin, slice and serve.

Makes one 8-inch round cake.

CRUNCHY MUFFINS

Ingredients

1½ cups refined flour + for lining the tins

1 teaspoon baking powder

A pinch of salt

1 cup corn flakes

1 tablespoon fat

½ orange

½ cup butter/margarine

¾ cup brown sugar

1 egg

2-3 drops vanilla essence

¼ cup milk

Topping

¼ cup walnuts, shelled

⅓ cup brown sugar

½ teaspoon cinnamon powder

Method

1. Preheat an oven to 180°C/350°F/ Gas Mark 4. Sift the flour with

the baking powder and salt. Lightly crush the corn flakes with the help of a rolling pin. Similarly crush the walnuts.

2. Grease eight muffin tins with the fat. Fill individual tins with flour till the edges, remove all the flour and lightly bang the tins so that all the flour is removed from it except for a very fine layer.

3. Grate the rind of orange. Cream the butter, brown sugar and orange rind in a bowl with a wooden spoon till light and fluffy. Beat the egg lightly with vanilla essence.

4. Add the milk and egg to the butter-sugar mixture and mix well. Add the flour mixture and mix in a clockwise manner. Mix in the corn flakes. Correct the consistency, if required, by adding more milk.

5. Divide the mixture equally between the muffin tins.Combine the ingredients for the topping and sprinkle over the muffins.

6. Bake in the preheated oven for fifteen to twenty minutes or till the skewer comes out clean from the muffin. Serve warm.

LOW-FAT BROWNIES

Ingredients

3 tablespoons unsweetened cocoa powder

1 cup refined flour

½ teaspoon baking powder

½ teaspoon soda bicarbonate

1 cup caster sugar

½ cup skimmed milk

2 egg whites, beaten

1 teaspoon vanilla essence

1½ tablespoons oil

Method

1. Preheat an oven to 180°C/350°F/ Gas Mark 4.

2, Line an eight-inch square cake tin with greaseproof paper.

3. Sift together the cocoa powder, flour, baking powder and soda bicarbonate into a bowl.

4. Stir in the caster sugar and beat in the milk, egg whites, vanilla essence and oil until thoroughly combined.

5. Pour the mixture into the prepared tin.
6. Bake for about twenty-five minutes, or until just firm to the touch.
7. Remove from the oven and leave in the tin until completely cold.
8. Cut into squares and remove gently from the tin with a spatula.

Makes 16 brownies

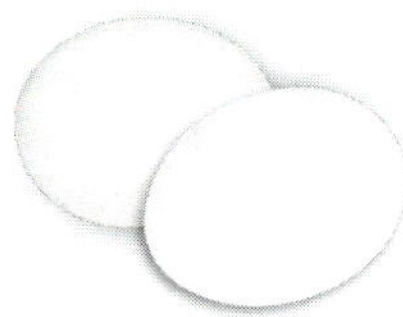

EGGLESS BROWNIES

Ingredients

100 grams dark chocolate, grated

1 1/3 cups refined flour

2 teaspoons baking powder

130 grams butter

1 cup + 1 ½ tablespoons caster sugar

1 teaspoon vanilla essence

½ cup walnut kernels, chopped

Method

1. Preheat an oven to 180°C/350°F/ Gas Mark 4. Grease an eight-inch square cake tin.

2. Sift together the flour and baking powder.

3. Melt the chocolate and butter in a double-boiler, or in a large microwave-safe bowl, uncovered, in the microwave oven on HIGH (100%) for one minute.

4. Beat in the sugar and vanilla essence and blend well.
5. Add the sifted flour and walnuts and mix well.
6. Pour the mixture into the tin and bake for twenty-five to thirty minutes.
7. Remove from the oven and place on a wire rack to cool.
8. Cut into squares and serve.

Makes 16 brownies

EGGLESS FRUIT CAKE

Ingredients

1 cup refined flour

¾ teaspoon soda bicarbonate

¾ teaspoon baking powder

1 tablespoon orange peel, hopped

1 tablespoon candied fruit, chopped

1 tablespoon sugar

4 tablespoons unsalted butter

½ tin condensed milk

A little less than ½ cup soda water

½ teaspoon vanilla essence

Method

1. Heat an oven to 150°C/300°F/ Gas Mark 2. Grease a baking tin and lightly dust it with flour.
2. Sift the flour with soda bicarbonate and baking powder. Add the chopped orange peel and candied fruit.
3. Beat together sugar and butter well; add the condensed milk and beat well.
4. Add the soda water, mix well and add the essence.

5. Gradually add the flour, beating well after each addition.
6. Beat well for three to four minutes till the mixture is smooth and light.
7. Pour into the prepared tin and bake in the preheated oven for about thirty to forty minutes.
8. Remove from the oven and place on a wire rack to cool.
9. Slice and serve.

CHOCOLATE CHIP COOKIES

Ingredients

¾ cup chocolate chips

¾ cup refined flour

60 grams low fat butter

1 egg white

½ teaspoon vanilla essence

½ teaspoon soda bicarbonate

¼ teaspoon salt

5 teaspoons sugar

½ cup coarsely crushed walnut halves

Method

1. Preheat an oven to 180°C/350°F/ Gas Mark 4. Grease a baking tray.
2. Cream the butter in a bowl. Add the egg white and vanilla essence and continue to cream till light and fluffy.
3. Sift together the flour, soda bicarbonate and salt and fold into the butter mixture and mix well.
4. Reserve a few chocolate chips and mix the rest with the sugar

and walnuts into the cookie dough. Divide the dough into twelve equal portions and shape each one into a round cookie.

5. Place the cookies a little apart on the greased baking tray.

6. Sprinkle the remaining chocolate chips on top and bake for twenty to twenty-five minutes.

7. Remove from the oven and transfer the cookies to a wire rack to cool. Store in an airtight container.

Makes 12 cookies

CHEESE CRISPIES

Ingredients

3 tablespoons grated processed cheese

1¼ cups refined flour, sifted

60 grams butter, softened

1 egg

1 teaspoon sugar

½ teaspoon salt

A pinch of paprika

A pinch of nutmeg

2 tablespoons cream

Method

1. Preheat an oven to 200°C/400°F/Gas Mark 6. Grease a baking tray.
2. Mix together the grated cheese, butter, egg, sugar, salt, paprika, nutmeg and cream in a bowl.
3. Add the flour and mix into a dough.
4. Roll out the dough into a half-inch thick rectangle on a lightly floured surface.

5. Cut into nine-inch long and half-inch wide strips, twist and place a little apart on the greased baking tray.

6. Bake for about fifteen minutes or until pale golden brown.

7. Remove from the oven and transfer to a wire rack to cool. Store in an airtight container.

Makes 15 nine-inch-long straws

JAMMIE BODGERS

Ingredients

2 cups refined flour

125 grams frozen butter, chopped

¼ cup + 1 tablespoon caster sugar

1 egg, lightly beaten

1 teaspoon vanilla essence

Filling

50 grams unsalted butter, softened

½ cup icing sugar

4-5 tablespoons strawberry jam

Method

1. Sift the flour into a bowl and rub the butter in with your fingertips. Add the sugar, egg and vanilla essence and mix into a soft dough. Knead the dough gently on a lightly floured surface until smooth.

2. Preheat an oven to 180°C/350°F/Gas Mark 4. Grease two baking trays.

3. Roll out the dough thinly on a lightly floured surface and cut into rounds with a two and

a half inch cutter. Re-roll the trimmings and cut into more rounds. You should get around thirty rounds.

4. Place fifteen rounds on a baking tray. With a small three-fourth inch heart-shaped cookie cutter cut out the centres of the remaining rounds. Place the cut-out rounds on the second baking tray.
5. Bake in the preheated oven for about twelve minutes or until pale golden. Remove from the oven and transfer the cookies to wire racks to cool completely.
6. For the filling, beat together butter and sugar until smooth and creamy. Spread the butter cream evenly on the whole cookies. Spoon a little jam over the butter cream and place the cut-out cookies on top, pressing gently so that the jam fills the heart-shaped space.

Makes 15 Jammie Bodgers

SHREWSBURY BISCUITS

Ingredients

1½ cups refined flour

125 grams butter

¾ cup caster sugar

2 egg yolks

Grated rind of 1 lemon

Method

1. Preheat an oven to 180°C/350°F/ Gas Mark 4. Grease two large baking trays.
2. Cream the butter and sugar until light and fluffy. Add the egg yolks and beat well.
3. Stir in the flour and grated lemon rind and mix to a fairly firm dough.
4. Turn out the dough onto a lightly floured surface and knead lightly till smooth. Roll the

dough out into a one-eighth-inch thick circle.

5. Cut into rounds with a two and a half inch round cookie cutter.
6. Place the rounds a little apart on the greased baking trays. Bake for about fifteen minutes, or until the biscuits are firm and a very light brown.
7. Remove from the oven and transfer to a wire rack to cool completely. Store in an airtight container.

Makes 15 biscuits

JEERA BISCUITS

Ingredients

2 tablespoons cumin seeds

2 cups refined flour

1½ teaspoons salt

1 teaspoon baking powder

¼ cup powdered sugar

½ cup oil

1 egg, lightly beaten

Method

1. Preheat an oven to 180°C/350°F/ Gas Mark 4. Grease a baking tray. Sift together the flour, salt and baking powder; mix in the cumin seeds.

2. In a large bowl, mix together the sugar and oil; add the egg and mix well. Add the flour mixture to the egg mixture and mix; add two tablespoons of water and knead into a soft dough.

3. Divide the dough into twenty equal portions. Roll each

portion into a ball and flatten slightly.

4. Place a little apart on the greased baking tray. Bake for about ten to fifteen minutes, or until light brown.

5. Remove from the oven and transfer the biscuits to a wire rack to cool. Store in an airtight container.

Makes 20 biscuits

HONEY, FIG AND WALNUT COOKIES

Ingredients

2 tablespoons honey

7 dried figs, finely chopped

5-6 walnut kernels, chopped

½ cup butter or margarine

1/8 cup brown sugar

5 dried dates, finely chopped

¼ teaspoon vanilla essence

¼ teaspoon cinnamon powder

¼ teaspoon clove powder

A small pinch of salt

½ teaspoon soda bicarbonate

1 egg

7/8 cup refined flour

90 grams rolled (porridge) oats

Method

1. Preheat an oven to 180°C/350°F/ Gas Mark 4. Grease a baking tray.
2. Cream the butter in a bowl. Add the dried figs and brown sugar and continue to beat well. Stir in the honey.
3. In a separate bowl, mix together the chopped dates, vanilla essence, cinnamon and clove powders, a pinch of salt and the soda bicarbonate.
4. In a third bowl, beat the egg well. Add the date and spice mixture and mix. Add the fig mixture and mix well.
5. Fold in the walnuts and flour and, finally, the rolled oats.
6. Place tablespoons of batter on the greased baking tray, with enough space in between. Bake in the preheated oven for twenty to twenty five minutes.
7. Remove from the oven and place the cookies on a wire rack to cool. Store in an airtight container.

CRUNCHY PEANUT COOKIES

Ingredients

½ cup peanut butter

2 tablespoons crushed roasted peanuts

¾ cup + 1 tablespoon refined flour

¼ teaspoon soda bicarbonate

½ teaspoon cinnamon powder

¾ cup + 1 tablespoon caster sugar

½ cup rolled (porridge) oats

¼ cup + 1 tablespoon desiccated coconut

1 teaspoon grated lemon rind

1 tablespoon golden syrup

Method

1. Preheat an oven to 180°C/350°F/Gas Mark 4. Grease a baking tray.
2. Sift together the flour, soda bicarbonate and cinnamon powder into a bowl. Add the sugar, oats, desiccated coconut

and lemon rind and mix well. Add the peanut butter, crushed peanuts, golden syrup and approximately two tablespoons of water and mix into a soft dough. Knead gently on a lightly floured surface until smooth. Wrap the dough in cling film and refrigerate for about thirty minutes.

3. Divide the dough in half and roll out each half between sheets of greaseproof paper into a quarter-inch thick rectangle. Cut into rounds with a two-and-a-half-inch round cookie cutter. Place well apart on the baking tray. Bake for about fifteen minutes or until light golden brown.

4. Remove from the oven and transfer the cookies to a wire rack to cool. Store in an airtight container.

Makes 35 cookies

MELTING MOMENTS

Ingredients

1¼ cups refined flour

110 grams butter

½ cup caster sugar

1 egg, beaten

½ teaspoon vanilla or almond essence

¾ teaspoon baking powder

1½ cups cornflakes

Method

1. Preheat an oven to 180°C/350°F/ Gas Mark 4. Grease a baking tray.
2. Cream together the butter and sugar in a bowl. Add the egg and the essence and mix well. Sift the flour with the baking powder and fold into the mixture. Mix to make a dough. Divide the dough into sixteen equal portions and roll into balls.
3. Spread the cornflakes on a sheet of greaseproof paper and roll the balls in them till evenly coated. Place the balls a little apart on the baking tray. Bake for fifteen to twenty minutes or until light brown.
4. Remove from the oven and set aside to cool slightly before transferring to a wire rack to cool. Store in an airtight container.

Makes 16 cookies

COCONUT KISSES

Ingredients

1¼ cups desiccated coconut

3 egg whites

1/8 teaspoon salt

1 cup caster sugar

1 teaspoon vanilla essence

Method

1. Preheat an oven to 170°C/325°F/ Gas Mark 3. Grease and flour a baking tray.
2. Beat the egg whites with salt until stiff. Add the sugar gradually, beating continuously. Fold in the vanilla essence and desiccated coconut.
3. Drop the batter in small mounds a little apart onto the baking tray. Bake for about forty to forty-five minutes. Remove from the oven and transfer to a wire rack to cool. Store in an airtight container.

Makes 35 cookies

MUSHROOM QUICHE

Ingredients

Pastry Crust

1 recipe Basic Shortcrust Pastry (page 92)

Filling

225 grams fresh button mushrooms, thinly sliced

1 tablespoon olive oil

½ tablespoon butter

1 garlic clove, crushed

½ tablespoon lemon juice

Salt to taste

Black pepper powder to taste

1 tablespoon fresh coriander, finely chopped

2 eggs

¾ cup fresh cream

¼ cup grated processed cheese

Method

1. Preheat a oven to 190°C/375°F/ Gas Mark 5.

2. Roll out the shortcrust pastry dough into a quarter-inch thick round and line a nine-inch round tart tin with it.

3. Trim the edges and prick the base all over with a fork.

4. For the filling, heat the olive oil and butter in a pan over medium heat; stir in the mushrooms, garlic and lemon juice.

5. Add the salt and pepper powder and cook until the mushrooms dry out. Increase the heat and cook until the mixture is dry.

6. Add the fresh coriander and adjust the seasoning. Whisk the eggs and cream together and stir in the mushroom mixture.

7. Sprinkle the cheese over the base of the tart and pour the mushroom filling over it.

8. Bake in the preheated oven for about thirty-five minutes, or until puffed up and golden brown. Cut into wedges and serve warm.

Makes one 9-inch quiche

BROWNIE CHEESECAKE

Ingredients

100 grams dark chocolate
1 cup refined flour
1 teaspoon baking powder
90 grams butter
¾ cup caster sugar
2 eggs
1 teaspoon vanilla essence
½ cup walnut halves, chopped
Oil for greasing

Filling

1 tablespoon unflavoured gelatine
225 grams unsalted cheese spread
⅔ cup yogurt
7 tablespoons sugar
1 teaspoon vanilla essence
2 egg whites

Method

1. Preheat an oven to 180°C/350°F/ Gas Mark 4. Grease an eight-inch round springform cake tin.
2. Sift the flour and baking powder together. Combine the chocolate and butter in a large microwave-safe bowl and cook, uncovered, for one minute on HIGH (100%)

till soft; alternatively melt the chocolate and butter together in a double-boiler.

3. Beat in the sugar, eggs and vanilla essence and mix well. Fold in the sifted flour and walnuts and mix well. Pour the mixture into the prepared cake tin and bake for forty-five minutes. Leave to cool in the tin.
4. To make the filling, place the gelatine in a bowl, add five tablespoons of water and leave to stand for two to three minutes. Stand the bowl over a pan of simmering water and stir until the gelatine dissolves completely. Leave to cool slightly.
5. Beat the cheese spread, yogurt, sugar and vanilla essence together in a separate bowl. Stir in the dissolved gelatine till well mixed. Whisk the egg whites in a clean bowl till stiff and fold into the cheese mixture. Spoon the mixture over the brownie base in the tin and level the surface. Chill in a refrigerator for at least four hours, or until set.
6. Remove the cheesecake carefully from the tin and transfer to a serving plate. Cut into wedges and serve.

Makes one 8-inch cheesecake

STRAWBERRY CHEESECAKE

Ingredients

500 grams strawberries, hulled

2 cups grated skimmed milk cottage cheese

3 tablespoons butter

1½ cups crumbled digestive biscuits

1 tablespoon gelatine

1½ cups drained skimmed milk yogurt

4 2/3 teaspoons sugar

Method

1. Melt the butter and add to crumbled biscuits and mix. Line the base of a six-inch round loose-bottomed cake tin with the mixture. Press the mixture lightly and place it in the refrigerator to set.

2. Reserve a few strawberries and purée the rest.

3. Mix the gelatine in a little water and place it in the microwave oven for fifteen seconds.

Remove from the microwave and set aside.

4. Place the drained yogurt in a bowl. Add the cottage cheese and mix with a whisk. Add the strawberry purée, Sugar Free Natura and blend with the hand blender.

5. Add the dissolved gelatine and blend again.

6. Strain and pour the mixture over the biscuit layer. Refrigerate for two to three hours.

7. Remove the cheesecake from the tin and garnish with the remaining strawberries. Cut into wedges with a sharp knife dipped in hot water and serve immediately.

CHEESE AND SPRING ONION TARTS

Ingredients

Pastry Crust

1 recipe of Basic Shortcrust Pastry (page 92)

Filling

½ cup grated processed cheese

3 spring onions, chopped

2 tablespoons olive oil

4-5 garlic cloves, chopped

1 cup White Sauce (see below)

1½ cups chopped spring onion greens

Salt to taste

½ teaspoon white pepper powder

Method

1. Preheat an oven to 200°C/400°F/ Gas Mark 6.
2. Roll out the pastry dough into a half-inch thick round on a

lightly floured surface. Using a three-inch round biscuit cutter, stamp out twelve rounds and line twelve tart tins.

3. Trim the excess dough and press lightly. Prick the pastry all over with a fork. Refrigerate the tart tins for ten minutes.

4. Bake the tarts for fifteen minutes, or till the crust is firm. Remove from the oven.

5. Heat the olive oil in a pan; add the garlic and sauté for two minutes. Add the spring onions and sauté till translucent. Stir in the white sauce and mix well.

6. Add the spring onion greens and season with salt and white pepper.

7. Remove from heat and spoon the filling into the tarts while they are warm.

8. Sprinkle grated cheese and bake for another five to six minutes and serve hot.

Makes 12 tarts

White Sauce

To make white sauce, melt 1 tablespoon of butter over low heat. Add 1 tablespoon of refined flour and sauté lightly till fragrant. Add 1 cup of lukewarm milk in a slow trickle, stirring continuously with a wire whisk, so that no lumps are formed. Cook till thick.

Makes 1½ cup white sauce

SPINACH AND CHEESE PIE

Ingredients

Pastry Crust

2 recipes Basic Shortcrust Pastry (page 92)

Filling

500 grams fresh spinach, stems removed

1 tablespoon olive oil

2 small onions, chopped

½ teaspoon dried oregano

Freshly ground black pepper powder to taste

Salt to taste

A pinch of grated nutmeg

½ cup cream

½ cup milk

2 eggs

225 grams cottage cheese, grated

Method

1. Preheat an oven to 180°C/350°F/ Gas Mark 4.

2. Cut the spinach leaves into thin ribbons with a sharp knife.

3. Heat the oil in a large pan; add the onions and sauté over medium heat for five minutes or until softened. Add the spinach, oregano, pepper powder, salt and nutmeg and cook over high heat, stirring frequently for about five minutes, or until most of the liquid has evaporated. Remove from heat and set aside to cool.

4. To make the custard, whisk together the cream, milk, one egg and a pinch of salt.

5. Divide the shortcrust pastry into two equal portions and roll out

each portion into a quarter-inch thick round.

6. Line an eight-inch round pie dish with one round of rolled-out pastry and trim the edges. Prick with a fork all over and refrigerate for ten minutes. Bake blind for twenty-five minutes.

7. Spread the spinach mixture in the pastry case and top it with the cottage cheese. Pour the custard mixture over it.

8. Cover the pie with the second pastry round and trim the edges. Pierce the pastry cover at intervals to allow the steam to escape. Use the pastry trimmings to create a design around the edge.

9. Beat the remaining egg and brush the top of the pie with it. Bake for fifty to sixty minutes till golden brown.

10. Cut into wedges and serve hot.

Makes one 8-inch pie

Note: Whenever you cover such a dish with pastry dough make sure that you make some holes in it called chimneys for steam to escape, prevent the base from getting soggy, and retain the shape of the pie.

BASIC FATLESS SPONGE CAKE

Ingredients

1 cup refined flour, sifted

Butter for greasing

4 eggs

½ cup + 2 tablespoons powdered sugar

1 teaspoon vanilla essence

Method

1. Preheat an oven to 180°C/350°F/Gas Mark 4. Line an eight-inch round cake tin and grease it well. Beat together the eggs, sugar and vanilla essence till light and creamy.
2. Gradually fold in the flour, stirring with a light hand only in one direction.
3. Pour into the prepared tin and bake for twenty-five to thirty minutes.
4. Remove from the oven and turn out onto a wire rack to cool completely.

Makes 400 grams

BASIC SPONGE CAKE

Ingredients

1 cup refined flour, sifted

50 grams butter

4 eggs

½ cup + 2 tablespoons sugar

1 teaspoon vanilla essence

Method

1. Preheat an oven to 180°C/350°F/ Gas Mark 4. Line and grease an eight-inch round cake tin.
2. Melt the butter and set it aside to cool. Beat together the eggs, sugar and vanilla essence till light and creamy. Gradually fold in the flour, stirring with a light hand only in one direction. Stir in the melted butter.
3. Pour into the prepared tin and bake in the preheated oven for twenty-five to thirty minutes, till well-risen and golden brown on top.
4. Turn out onto a wire rack and leave to cool completely before icing it.

EGGLESS SPONGE CAKE

Ingredients

1 cup refined flour

1½ teaspoons soda bicarbonate

1½ teaspoons baking powder

3 tablespoons sugar

55 grams unsalted butter

½ tin (200 grams) condensed milk

1 cup milk

1 teaspoon vanilla essence

Method

1. Preheat an oven to 180°C/350°F/ Gas Mark 4. Grease an eight-inch round cake tin and lightly dust it with flour.
2. Sift the flour with soda bicarbonate and baking powder. Cream together the sugar and butter till light and fluffy.
3. Add the condensed milk and beat well. Stir in the milk and vanilla essence.

4. Gradually add the flour, mixing well after each addition. Mix well for three to four minutes till the mixture is smooth and light.

5. Pour the batter into the prepared tin and bake for about thirty to thirty-five minutes.

6. Remove from the oven and turn out onto a wire rack and leave to cool completely.

Makes 450 grams

Note: To grease a cake tin, apply melted butter or oil evenly and sprinkle with refined flour. Turn over the tin, tap it to shake off excess flour.

BUTTER ICING

Ingredients

90 grams butter, softened

2 cups icing sugar, sifted

1 teaspoon vanilla essence

Method

1. Mix together the butter, icing sugar and vanilla essence in a bowl until smooth. Use as required.

Note: 1) This makes sufficient icing to cover an eight-inch round cake.
2) Use butter icing on cakes and to sandwich cookies.

BASIC SHORTCRUST PASTRY

Ingredients

1 cup refined flour

60 grams butter, chilled, chopped

Method

1. Place the flour and butter in a food processor and process until the mixture resembles coarse breadcrumbs.
2. If mixing by hand, rub the butter into the flour with your fingertips.
3. With the processor running, add drops of iced water until the dough comes together.
4. If not using a processor, mix in the iced water with a knife or a wooden spoon.
5. You can mix the dough by hand without handling the dough too much.
6. You will need approximately two and a half tablespoons of water.
7. Press the dough into a ball, wrap in a greaseproof paper or cling film and refrigerate for at

least thirty minutes before rolling or shaping.

8. Shortcrust pastry can be stored in a refrigerator for two days, or in the freezer for up to three months.

Makes enough for one 9-inch pastry base.

BISCUIT CRUMB PASTRY

Ingredients

2 cups finely crushed biscuits (such as digestive, ginger or plain)

75 grams butter, melted

½ teaspoon grated nutmeg

Method

1. Preheat an oven to 190°C/375°F/ Gas Mark 5. Mix together the crushed biscuits, butter and nutmeg thoroughly with a wooden spoon.
2. Press the mixture into a nine-inch pie dish and build it up the sides, making sure that the edges are neat.
3. Bake for five minutes. Leave to cool in the dish. Fill the pastry case with a filling of your choice. Makes enough for one 9-inch pastry base

Note: You can use this pastry as a base for cheesecakes, soufflés and fruit flans.

TABLES

OVEN TEMPERATURE CHART

CELSIUS	FAHRENHEIT	GAS MARK	DESCRIPTION
110	225	quarter (¼)	very cool
130	250	half (½)	-
140	275	1	cool
150	300	2	-
170	325	3	very moderate
180	350	4	moderate
190	375	5	-
200	400	6	moderately hot
220	425	7	hot
230	450	8	-
240	475	9	very hot

MEASURING CUPS AND SPOONS

MEASURES	VOLUME
1 tablespoon	15 ml
2 teaspoons	10 ml
1 teaspoon	5 ml
½ teaspoon	2.5 ml
¼ teaspoon	1.25 ml
1 cup	200 ml
½ cup	100 ml
¼ cup	50 ml
⅓ cup	65 ml

GLOSSARY

English	Hindi
Almond	badam
Apple	saeb
Banana	kela
Butter	makkhan
Buttermilk	chhaach
Cardamoms, green	chhoti elaichi
Carrot	gajar
Cinnamon	dalchini
Cloves	laung
Coconut, desiccated	khopra ka sookha choora
Coriander, fresh	hara dhania
Cottage cheese	paneer
Cream	malai
Cumin seeds	jeera
Currants	mannuca
Dates, dried	chhuare
Egg white	ande ka jarda
Eggs	anda
Fig	anjeer
Garlic cloves	lehsun ki kaliyan

English	Hindi
Honey	shahad/madhu
Lemon	nimbu
Mushrooms	dhingri/khumb/ guchhi/kukurmutta
Nutmeg	jaiphal
Oats	jaee
Olives	jaitun
Orange	narangi
Peanuts	moongphali
Peppercorns, black	kali mirch
Peppercorns, white	safed mirch
Pineapple	ananas
Raisins	kishmish
Refined flour	maida
Spinach, fresh	palak ke taze patte
Spring onion greens	hare pyaaz ki pattiyan
Spring onions	hara pyaaz
Walnut	akhrot
Yogurt	dahi